I0837742

THE FOUR PILLARS OF CAMPAIGN VICTORY

HOW TO PREPARE YOURSELF TO RUN FOR OFFICE AND WIN

JAMES PAUL FISHER & J. WESLEY FISHER

First Edition, 2020

ISBN 9798638176327

Cataloging-in-Publication data on file with the Library of Congress

Disclaimer: The advice and strategies found within may not be suitable for every situation. This work is sold with the understanding that neither the author nor the publisher are held responsible for the results accrued from the advice in this book. Nothing in this book should be considered legal advice

CONTENTS

INTRODUCTION

Seeking and ultimately holding a popularly elected office is one of the most important ways for an American to observe the obligations of citizenship. Moreover, the experience can be a humbling opportunity to work for one's fellow citizens in the sphere of public service. While many have failed as candidates, and failed as elected officers, many more have sacrificed a great deal of time and personal energy in the sincere effort of helping their communities, states, and our nation by serving in public office.

At the founding of our country, George Mason famously remarked that many of those in attendance at the constitutional convention were insincere "office hunters." There have always been those who will betray the seat that they may happen to hold by election. This is a sad reality of our republic. However, another reality is that there are many who are willing to honestly serve, and many more who should be encouraged to serve due to the talents and energy that they would bring to office. It is for them that this book is intended.

The pillars in this book are an assemblage of the primary and core political components of a winning campaign. In an ideal campaign, each pillar, along with its subsidiary elements, would all be encompassed in your strategy. While there are no guarantees in life, the proper observance of these pillars has historically led to political victory. Conversely, the failure to observe the concepts in this book will very likely result in a poor campaign and a loss on Election Day.

A campaign is like an engine with multiple component parts. Each part fulfills a valuable function for the overall robust operation of the engine. While it is possible to have an occasional malfunction and keep the engine running, the more elements of a campaign that fail, the more likely the engine itself will fail. The campaign should be pursued from the ideal. The successful candidate should attempt to make sure all the pistons are firing and that the machine is finely tuned. All moving parts should be orchestrated to work together in unison and harmony. The more this ideal is achieved, the more likely the candidate will prevail on Election Day.

Campaigning, even in a small local race is tantamount to a full time job because the concepts described in this book require extraordinary time and money. Thus, the decision to run for office is not one to be entered into lightly. Rather, the decision to run should be well considered over time with due regard for the rigors that a political campaign brings. To do this, a successful candidate will enter a political race deliberately and with a spirit of service. The rewards of service need to be reward enough and it is that spirit that will guide and sustain the successful candidate through the days, weeks, and months of a political campaign.

THE ORIGIN OF A CAMPAIGN

The first step in a campaign is the potential candidate's decision to run for a particular office. This sounds easy enough, but it should be a weighty decision made after a great deal of consideration. A new candidate for public office will rarely know what lies ahead in a campaign. At most, the novice will possess several assumptions based largely upon what has been observed from a distance. These assumptions are often faulty, ill-considered, and bolstered by the potential candidate's blind ambition to run. The best thing one can do is to slow down and maturely appraise what lies ahead by seeking advice, counsel and studying the realities of campaigning from credible sources of information.

In reality, running for office is both grueling and unpredictable. In many ways it is like sailing into the dawn of what appears to be a beautiful day. The day seems tranquil enough at the beginning, but it inevitably will involve waves, potential rough seas, torrential storms and the ever-present threat of capsizing. A campaign can only weather so many storms.

Campaigns always begin with pleasant weather, but as time wears on, conditions always change. Your opponent and his or her surrogates will become more hostile, the once friendly news media will hit you with an unflattering story with limited or no advance notice, or even more likely, you will experience troubles inside your own political camp. Personality clashes among volunteers or staffers, funding difficulties and other internal issues will no doubt crop up during a campaign. Moreover, a potential candidate continues to be human with all the attendant difficulties of human life. Bills need to be paid, family members continue to have a life and want you to be involved, and unless you are independently wealthy, you may have a job that requires you to actually show up at the office and work. The successful candidate will have anticipated these issues during the decision-making process either intuitively, but more likely based upon good advice from those who know the promises and perils of running for office. The final decision is yours, but it should be the result of an investigatory, collaborative process where you genuinely consider the advice and opinions of others, especially those closest to you in your daily life.

TEN QUESTIONS TO ASK YOURSELF WHEN DECIDING TO RUN FOR OFFICE

Your decision to run, or not, should be predicated upon many factors. This section will explore ten questions you should ask yourself to determine if you are ready to run for office:

1. Am I Familiar Enough with the Office I Am Seeking?
2. Are my Closest Friends and Family Supportive?
3. Do I Have the Personal Resources?
4. Can I Raise the Money?
5. Should I Position Myself as an Insider or Outsider?
6. Am I Letting My Ego Cloud My Decision to Run?
7. Am I Familiar with My Universe of Voters?
8. Is the Seat I am Seeking Open or Occupied?
9. Should I Consider a Springboard First
10. Can I Wait?

Am I Familiar Enough with the Office I Am Seeking?

Among the considerations is whether you really know the office you seek. From the outside looking in it may seem that the knowledge requirements of the office are simple. Truthfully, participation in governmental offices at all levels has become laden with legal parameters and requirements. Simplicity in the job is rarely the case for a public official. This is evidenced by the fact that almost all public offices will have some local, state, or federal legal officer that advises the public officials on the legal issues that are involved in their public service. By way of example, local offices will no doubt involve matters of zoning, budgets, and public safety. State offices will require an elected official to be cognizant of the state constitution and state law. Federal offices involve an unbelievable array of laws, regulations, and agencies upon which the setting of public policy may require a vote from a publicly elected official. If you seek to challenge an incumbent, you better believe that the incumbent already knows these things and will highlight their superior knowledge of the legalities of the office. In an open seat election, the prepared candidate will demonstrate to the voter that he or she has a firm grasp on the types of policy issues that will be faced during their public service.

Knowing the office you seek not only creates self-confidence in a potential candidate's decision to run, it also will be readily apparent to potential supporters and voters. If you have experience in the general operations of the particular office that you are considering, this factor will weigh heavily in favor of a decision to run. If however, you honestly feel that you will have to study up on the office in order to credibly run for the position as well as to serve if elected, this would suggest that you may not be ready, or that the office is not for you. It is only one factor, but it is important. Any inexperience can and will be sniffed out by your opponent and exploited in their favor and against your candidacy. And, in the event your lack of experience is put on full display for the electorate to see, it can doom your campaign to failure.

Knowing the office you seek, and being qualified for such office should also constitute a personal gauge on the sincerity of your desire to actually serve. Wanting to serve, if nothing else should mean that you honestly feel that your experience and knowledge will help others. If you are not actually confident in your experience, then your desire to hold the particular office is likely more due to your desire to hold public office for your own pleasure rather than for the benefit of the citizens you would be serving.

Are my Closest Friends and Family Supportive?

The next criteria in the decision to run is the determination of whether your immediate support group can not only support you, but also give the personal commitment or investment needed for a successful campaign effort. The necessary support of your immediate family members cannot be understated. First, one stark reality of public office is that, even in the candidacy for the office, there is much that is truly public and very little that is private. You and your family members need to analyze this prospect with clear minds and open eyes. Of course, the level of public scrutiny is proportionate to the level of office you seek, but even the local office holder will often be in the local newspaper. Your local campaign will be fodder for local news print, and even in an online world, news organizations require content. Political campaigns are great content generators for any news organization. Thus, your family members must know that you will be thrust, to some degree, into the public arena. This in turn means, even in small localities, that family members will be associated with the candidate and the office holder if you are elected. Your family must be willing to accept this lifestyle change and be supportive of the notion that you will be scrutinized. Moreover, you and they should be prepared to accept that such scrutiny may not always be fair.

It should be emphasized again that the level of scrutiny is very different depending upon the level of office you seek. A small town council race will clearly be much less intrusive for your family than a run for federal or statewide office. However, your kids, if you have any, go to school, your spouse goes to the store and to the kids activities in public places. They will be known and seen as your kids and spouse. Your child's school teacher or sports coach will ask your child "are you related to" you. Hopefully, the next report from your child is that something positive was said. The point is, that while a local office, or the campaign to achieve it, may not be intensely public, it is still public. In considering your run for office, this discussion must take place with your family. For that matter, extended family and close friends may need to be queried on their feelings about this if for no other reason than to prepare them for the concept of you having a public profile and putting them on notice of the types of things involved in the office you seek. This advance notice will better prepare them to support you in their own circles of influence.

Another consideration in family and friend support is that the light of a campaign can get hot. When you are under scrutiny as a candidate, the emotional support of family can be the tonic that gets you through to the next day. Without it, a candidate is in a tough situation trying to deal with the stress of campaign accusations or innuendos concerning you or your positions that may emerge during a campaign. In the decision of whether to run, you need to apprise your family of the need for support, and it can be crucial to get their sincere commitment. You want them to know this in advance rather than to discover it in the middle of your run for office.

Even in the best of times, campaigns involve a great deal of personal sacrifice. Much of this sacrifice is in the nature of time. In a family setting, as you likely know, your time also belongs, in part, to your family. When you give your time to the rigors of a campaign, you are taking it from them. That is a big deal. Most people, taking inventory of their life's activities, would place their child's school play or sports game as much more rewarding that the fundraiser they may have to attend because of a political campaign. Your family also needs advance notice of the time sacrifices that will attend your campaign so that they can make a conscious commitment to the sacrifice with a full awareness of the level of the sacrifice. Moreover, on many occasions their time will also be needed for your particular campaign event. In this scenario, not only are you giving your time, but you also are pledging the time of your family members and they are taking away their time from their own endeavors and committing it to you. The decision to run needs to factor family support into the "should I run" equation. Such support is their emotional commitment, privacy relinquishment and the precious resource of time. Lacking clarity on whether you will have such support weighs heavily against a run for public office. On the other hand, the full and informed support of your family will weigh in favor of running for the office in which you seek to serve.

Do I Have the Personal Resources?

There is a relative proportional ratio between what you need and the level of office for which you are considering a run. Your personal resources are time and money. While you can fundraise for the latter, which is no small challenge, you only have so many hours in the day to give to any particular endeavor. A decision to run for office should give great consideration to your personal resources and how they match up against the level of office you are seeking. All campaigning requires a time commitment. However, a local race will involve much less time than a state or federal office campaign. This of course, also depends in part upon the size of the electoral district in a given locality. A large county or city may have electoral districts that are similar in population size to state or federal offices. In such cases, the amount of personal resources needed are akin to such offices. A small town or county office is a different story. If you are interested in a run for office, a smaller electoral district is often a good first step into politics for fairly obvious reasons. In terms of resources, a smaller district campaign can be accommodated much more easily. A town council or county board member of a small jurisdiction can, and often is, made up of part time legislators who have full time jobs. Running for such offices can be done in the evenings and weekends and can even accommodate personal time being reserved for family activities. Of course, the more time you have on your hands, the more you can devote to any campaign, but if you have less available time, consider serving in a lower profile public office. Not only will your run for office have a greater chance of success, you also will gain the luxury of learning some things about the perils of politics in the shallow end of the pool where there is less danger.

The same can be said for money. The greater the office you seek, the more likely you will be successful in running for it if you are financially secure. Many people have observed that high level offices have a tendency of being filled by wealthy candidates. There is no mystery in this fact. If you have money, then you have the flexibility of being as politically active as you may desire. Of course this is not to say that only the wealthy are serving at high levels of government, but there is an undeniable natural tendency for members of the three branches of federal office to be filled with persons with little or no financial concerns.

Your decision to run for office should juxtapose the realities of your personal resources against the level of office you are seeking. If you are well suited with both time and money, then you are in a good position to devote your resources to most any office. If you have, like most people, limitations on your time and money, then consider the reality of the strain that a campaign can put on your resources depending upon the level of office you are considering. This is not to say that only the wealthy should run, but rather an acknowledgement that personal resources are a key consideration in your decision to mount what can be a very consuming political campaign for office. Your decision to run should be pragmatic and should honestly appraise your available personal resources.

Can I Raise the Money?

Another point for the potential candidate to consider is the prospective budget for a successful run for office. The pillars of electoral politics discussed herein can also serve as a checklist of items with each potentially carrying a price tag. In your decision to run, you must prepare a checklist of items that you feel are needed to communicate your political message to the given electoral universe. The sum total will likely be a bit less, in reality, to what you will actually need because there are always a handful of unanticipated costs. However, your budget will give you a ballpark figure with which you can ask yourself a difficult question. Can I raise this money?

If you doubt your ability to raise funds to the level of your budget, they it is likely that you will struggle in the campaign. On the other hand, if the sum total of your expected budget seems realistic given not only your personal resources but also the resources of your friends, likely supporters and others, then the analysis weighs in favor of pulling the trigger on a run for office.

Should I Position Myself as an Insider or Outsider?

Another factor in the decision of whether a run for office is right for you is the inescapable nature of provincial politics. This factor is especially important in local office elections. In smaller districts, counties or towns, voters are often distrustful of an outsider running for office. If you are new to the district and your likely opponent is an "old timer" that everyone knows, your run will be distinctly uphill. This does not mean that it is impossible to win, it is simply an important factor to weigh along with all the others. On the other hand, if you are an insider, or, perhaps better stated, a long-standing resident with strong community ties to the district, you will likely have a much easier time assembling a base of local support.

In many cases however, the opposite framework is in effect, and being an insider can become a political liability. This is most evident when there is considerable distrust or low public approval with the institution one is seeking election to. While this is often truer for state and federal offices such as races for U.S. Congress, which enjoys consistently dismal approval ratings, positioning oneself as an outsider with fresh ideas and experience has been successful in countless local races where the local political establishment has lost public favor due to something like an unpopular or poorly executed local project or program.

You should not shrink from running for an office from outside the network of people within the governmental system that houses that office, it is simply a factor to weigh in your decision-making process. Generally, the insider's path is the easier path, but you should make your decision to position yourself as an insider or outsider based on your personal qualities and principles as a candidate.

Am I Letting My Ego Cloud My Decision to Run?

*"When you are thinking of running for office,
don't let flattery and vague promises cloud your
analysis. If you let these vain passes at your ego
overwhelm your decision making, it is likely that
you will eventually find yourself alone on the
campaign ship with a tiny crew of supporters."*

The human ego is a required mental and emotional component, but it is also subject to manipulation. As the ego rises, rationality fades. It is against this concept that a potential candidate should be very cautious of the political operative who suggests that he or she would "make a great candidate." Tales of vulnerable incumbents and the wonder with which you would serve in office are the siren calls of the political naves who are more concerned with filling a ballot slate for their own reasons than for your success.

Any person who attempts to overly persuade you to run for office should be viewed with caution. Partisans seek candidates not necessarily because they can win. Rather, they often may seek to draw resources away from other threatening challenges by keeping an incumbent occupied with a nuisance opponent. Alternatively, you may be getting pressure to run from a person or persons who simply have "an axe to grind" with the incumbent in the particular seat. The question for you should be whether or not you wish to be a stooge for the purposes of others when it is going to be you on the political hot seat during the campaign. If you are approached for a run by a pushy political type, be careful to watch for flattery and promises of the grandeur of public office. While it is certainly possible that you are being sought for a legitimate campaign fight, it is also possible that you are being propped up in order to distract the attention of a particular incumbent on the "other side." One suggestion for handling this is to politely inquire as to what level of funding is being promised from the person or persons imploring you to run for office. In other words, find out if they are going to "put their money where their mouths are." If the money question is met with prevarication and uncertainly, then it may be that there is absolutely no intention of providing any support to your campaign.

When you are thinking of running for office, don't let flattery and vague promises cloud your analysis. If you let these vain passes at your ego overwhelm your decision making, it is likely that you will eventually find yourself alone on the campaign ship with a tiny crew of supporters. When the numbers come in on Election Day delivering a walloping win for the other side, there will be just enough holes on board the ship in which the rats will run to hide. Be your own person from the beginning to the end of your political career. In so doing, you will be far more successful not only in campaigning, but also in serving the office you hold.

Am I Familiar with My Universe of Voters?

In the business of electoral politics, you will often hear the word "universe." This is the term that is typically used for the number of registered voters in the district in which you are considering a run for office. It is within this universe in which you must communicate and otherwise work politically to get elected. Each public office is apportioned with a number of registered voters and, depending on the size and type of jurisdiction you are in, the universe of voters can be dramatically different in both size and demographics. In considering a run for office, a candidate must find out the number of registered voters with whom he or she must communicate their electoral message. The larger the district, the more the previously described resources will be needed for a successful run for office. Additionally, larger offices tend to draw even greater public scrutiny and intrusiveness into ones private life. On the other hand if your universe is the number of voters in a small town, then the opposite is true.

Once you have discovered your total universe, your decision to run will also be affected by the reality of voter turnout. The universe of likely voters is a must know in your decision making process. Not only are voters inconsistent in their voting habits, there are different voter turnout likelihoods or "turnout models" for different election cycles. In a presidential election year, a much higher number of voters will turn out to vote. Some states have elections every year. A gubernatorial year will have a bit lesser turnout. A congressional year perhaps a bit less than gubernatorial, and a local election year will have the tiniest universe of likely voters. So, for example, in a small town of ten thousand voters, a local election for public office may be decided on a voter turnout of ten percent. Finding and communicating with those ten percent will be less onerous, burdensome, expensive, or difficult than if your universe was the same town during a presidential election year with sixty five percent turnout. Of course a county office with five hundred thousand voters will involve much more resources in order to successfully run. This type of information is critical to your decision to run. Will the office you seek be subject to the turnout of a presidential year, a gubernatorial year, a congressional year, or a local year? Is your election district small or large? There are as many variations as there are states and localities in America. This is critical research that will affect your decision to run for office. The less voters that you need to contact, the easier the run for office will be and *vice versa*. If the potential run for office is relatively easy, then the decision to run is less difficult. Of course a relatively difficult run should make the decision process more profound and thorough.

Unlike the real universe, the political universe is subject to either reliability or volatility. Some voter universes remain constant over the years particularly if there has been little or no residential growth. Suburban areas adjacent to metropolitan areas are unique in this regard. As a general rule of thumb. Three percent annual residential growth will be a fairly reliable voter universe in terms of political viewpoints or ideology among the voters. As growth rates climb however, a particular voting district can become volatile and subject to change in ideology.

Is The Seat I am Seeking Open or Occupied?

As noted previously, there is a natural advantage for an aspiring candidate to seek the position of their former boss. "Inheriting" a seat comes with the advantages of incumbency. Given this fact, another consideration in whether you should run, particularly if you are an "outsider" is whether the seat you are considering is an open seat or a seat that is occupied with an incumbent office holder. The power of incumbency cannot be overstated. If you are considering running against an incumbent, not only should you consider all of the points in this book, you should really seek the advice of a credible political consultant who will be honest with you. The power of incumbency is huge. By way of example, It is routine for over ninety percent of congressional incumbents running for reelection to their office to be victorious. Of course, some incumbents deserve a challenge for a variety of reasons, but the question is, should you be the person treading against such difficult odds? An open seat is a different thing altogether. The point is that your decision should be all the more cautious if you are considering a run against an incumbent. An incumbent has plenty of advantages that a challenger does not have. First and foremost, they have a standing treasury with a list of known contributors who they can count on to fund their reelection effort. They also have an existing public platform from which to communicate with voters. They already hold the office, so it is expected that they communicate with voters on various issues within the parameters of the particular office and the policy issues involved therein. The incumbent will also have spent considerable time in the public eye such that they have the valuable political asset of name recognition. This is an asset that most challengers will have to pay for, and the price tag of mass communication with voters to raise name recognition is very expensive. In an open seat election, it is more likely that the candidates are on equal footing in these crucial areas. Absent the assistance of a departing incumbent, open seat contestants will scramble to develop an edge in each of these areas. Their relative political skills will determine who is able to gain such an edge and roll it into an Election Day victory.

In an occupied seat, your research should include reliable information and research on whether the incumbent is truly "vulnerable." While anecdotal information can be of some help, polling and opinion surveys will likely yield better data on the question of whether the incumbent is politically vulnerable to a challenge. An incumbent is typically vulnerable to electoral defeat in a few limited scenarios. First, if your incumbent is in a party in which a "wave election" takes place he or she may be swept out of office if the incumbent has a popularly known association with either an issue or a higher ticket candidate with extraordinary unpopularity. Election waves not only sweep candidates into office on the coattails of a popular higher ticket candidate, but they also can throw incumbents out of office in the same manner. Partisan association with high level incumbents who have developed political "negatives" or relative unpopularity tends to rub off on other members in the same party. This is particularly true when they have been seen together or photographed together often as political colleagues. Additionally, powerful issue identification can sweep members of a party either in or out of office depending upon whether the issue has gained popular momentum in either direction. Wave elections tend to be unpredictable in advance and unstoppable when they occur, but they constitute the exception in politics rather than the rule. It is possible however, through polling and reliable partisan intelligence to factor the potential for a wave election into your decision to run so it is something to consider if the winds seem to be gathering in such a direction.

Your decision on whether to run against an incumbent should also consider the potential for scandal. Again, this is the exception rather than the rule. However, it is possible to see in advance that some office holders have simply betrayed the trust of their office. Sometimes this has happened so often that scandals or the rumors of scandals may play a huge factor in a political rejection of the incumbent's reelection bid.

Should I Consider a Springboard First?

Another consideration in the decision to run for office is whether the office itself is just too much for your political experience. Most high level office holders began their political career by seeking lower level public offices. Once they gained political footing and some experience, they were in a much better position to analyze the decision to run for a relatively high office, or at least a higher one than they happen to hold at the time. A springboard public office which leads to higher office can be a valuable political mechanism. Assuming the good faith in your service in the springboard position, there is absolutely nothing unethical about using the advantages gained in your experience in one political office for the run toward a higher political office. In fact, it can be argued that lower level offices can be the "farm team" for higher office. Here you gain experience in the legalities and protocols of serving in government and will, in fact, be a better public servant in a higher office because of the experience that you have gained.

Can I Wait?

*"In deciding to run, consider this question. Can I
work closely with the current incumbent such that
when he or she retires or moves on with their career,
I can inherit the gravitas of their incumbency?"*

There is an age-old adage that in politics, "timing is everything." History proves this point time and time again when people seem to be in the right place at the right time and they practically stumble backwards into public office. Once in office, they use the power of incumbency to remain in office for a long time and even are able to use the particular office as a springboard to another even higher office. Your decision to run should assess whether there is a chance of gaining your office by preparation, proximity, and attrition.

It is the nature of life that all things have a cycle no matter how long it may seem to take. Elected officials do not remain in office forever though some do, of course, hold their office for a long time. In deciding to run, consider this question. Can I work closely with the current incumbent such that when he or she retires or moves on with their career, I can inherit the gravitas of their incumbency? Many office holders started off as legislative aides, campaign staffers or other loyal political supporters to an incumbent such that when the incumbent moved on, they moved in.

Waiting, and not mounting an aggressive campaign for a particular office, may in fact be the best and most reliable strategy in gaining public office. The value of serving in other roles in close proximity to the office holder in the seat you desire is great. First, you will have put yourself in a position to see if the service in office is something that you will actually enjoy by observing the current office holder. Second, you will learn valuable political tools from an incumbent who has already plowed the ground on which you are seeking to travel. As they say, there is no need "to reinvent the wheel." Take full advantage of an office holding mentor if you can find one in the arena in which you desire to serve. Also, being in proximity to an incumbent office holder will gain you an inside track to the incumbent's political support base. Of course, in the event the incumbent taps you to fill the seat that he or she is vacating, there will no doubt be an extended preparation period where you will be groomed for office and hand-delivered to the supporters of the incumbent. Incumbent office holders like the prospect of leaving behind an ostensibly loyal political legacy. It makes them feel as though they are leaving their constituency in good hands by having personally selected their successor in office. So, your decision to run for a particular office should include the analysis of whether you can gain the office through the natural process of attrition, either one you work with as an employee or volunteer, or one that you can get close to.

POPULARITY

"OR: Merkley Rally" by AFL-CIO Field is licensed under CC BY 2.0

Now that you have made the decision to run for office you are ready to learn the absolutely essential pillars of campaign victory. These pillars are key in every campaign and the more you understand and know their components, the more likely it is that you will win your election. The first pillar is a psychological concept which requires some elaboration.

We are, as adults, undeniably an older version of what we once were as children. Much of how we act as adults may involve some refinement and maturity, but in actuality, we have not changed that much since our school days. We want to be liked, and we like people who are likeable. The first pillar of campaign victory is a recognition of that reality.

The most popular person wins the election. We have a collective social tendency to adore the popular person. Our society is geared that way. Humanity is geared that way. Most political contests cannot escape this truism. Political consultants, regardless of party, will tell candidates that they must "be likeable," or that "the person with the most friends, wins." These are simply components of popularity. Since we were children, we have always wanted to be with "the in crowd." To be popular was, during childhood, the key to many superlatives. "Most likely to succeed" or the "King and Queen" of the prom. Our collective psyche has been mapped such that the popular person must somehow deserve to be voted into something because they are so damned cool! Scoff at this notion to your political peril.

You say, "No, wait a minute, we are mature and grown up now!" Right, we are really grown up in a world where our television set tells us who the best singer is, the best actor is, the best athlete is, so on and so forth in nearly nauseating detail. If you want to win political office, you must accept the reality that people want to vote for the person that other people view as popular. If you can create this impression in the mind of the electorate, you will be the winner of the election.

Popularity is thus the key pillar of electoral success, with the remaining pillars being the primarily accepted and required mechanisms to achieve superior popularity. Achieving superior popularity in the minds of people who don't know you and have never met you is the main challenge for a candidate. The campaign machinery, assuming it embraces the remaining pillars of victory, is the way you achieve superior popularity. There are also several political techniques that can help you achieve this goal.

THIRD PARTY CREDIBILITY

One fundamental technique in building an image of popularity is the use of what is often called "third party credibility." Various communication modes should employ the concept of third-party credibility which is the use of other people to vouch for what a great office holder you will be. The use of other people to sing your praises accomplished a number of things. First, it may be perceived as arrogant if one goes around telling everyone how great they are. You need other people to do that to avoid looking like an egomaniac. Second, the use of other people lends believability, particularly when they give examples of how your experience or leadership has affected their lives. People trust others to tell your story when they may not trust you so much. This device has been used with great success over the years where candidates have had others tell stories of how the candidate saved them, helped them, or achieved something arguably wonderful that changed the life of the third party. The use of third party supporters vouching for your candidacy also underscores the notion that other people like you and that therefore you are popular. The more people vouch for you, the more popular you will appear.

THE BANDWAGON EFFECT

The next level of third-party credibility is to increase the number of third party endorsers to as many people as possible. During the campaign, the image of popularity grows if nurtured correctly. The successful candidate will roll out endorsements on a continuing basis. These endorsement lists of supporters should grow week by week, month by month reaching a crescendo just prior to Election Day. The successful candidate will also use the right type of endorsements. In establishing and reinforcing popularity, the successful candidate not only produces ever climbing numbers of publishable endorsers, he or she also demonstrates their diverse appeal by showing off the types of endorsers in his or her camp. You must try to show that everybody likes you in order to be eminently popular. Throw in members of all political parties, organizations, belief systems, racial identities, and other backgrounds of diverse natures. You are trying to show that you are popular in a multi-dimensional way and that everyone likes you. Since everyone likes you, the voter should also. You are creating a band wagon effect and telling the voters that so many people like you, that you must be the popular person. Again, the popular person is adored, and thus will be the likely victor on Election Day.

These endorsements should not necessarily be political endorsements of other office holders who may have some positive attributes in your electoral universe. In reality, other politicians also carry negatives and you may inadvertently alienate voters who do not like the politicians who are endorsing you. There are far more valuable endorsements in your political universe, especially in a local election. The local chair of the district youth sports league, a revered, long-standing educator who taught multiple generations of voters, or the parent teacher association president are all the types of iconic local endorsements that you want to vouch for your candidacy. These are people who are known by many and often very well liked and popular. When they endorse you, they underscore the insinuation that you must be the popular candidate and thus are the one deserving of election. Unless you are running in a very partisan race, don't stress about asking your member of congress or another politician to endorse you. At any one time, nearly half the voters don't like them, so why risk turning off all those voters? Rather, remember that you need a significant number and a diverse nature of popular, likable icons in the district in which you are seeking to get elected. Their popularity will be attributed to you by association. And their ever-increasing numbers will create a band wagon effect where voters will be itching to proclaim that they are supporting you.

Okay, so now you understand the pillar of popularity and the methods of establishing it, what can you do in order to get this information out to the voting universe? Well, a good deal of this depends upon the available machinery in the other pillars of electoral victory discussed later in the book. For now, you should know that somehow you need to broadcast your popularity early, often and with increasing intensity as the campaign develops. Here are some tips that have worked for many candidates.

ACCUMULATING ENDORSEMENTS

Collect your endorsements by expressly asking for them along with permission to use the endorsers name and, if possible, a quotation about why they are supporting you for office. First, select the "low hanging fruit" of your friends and known supporters and then work on making voter contacts with community icons. As you earn support, expressly get the permission to use each voters name on any and all literature in the campaign. Some may not feel comfortable with that and you should scrupulously respect that fact being happy that they are at least voting for you. But with the others, collect names like you are filling a scrap book. All of these endorsements should ultimately be doled out in email blasts, or other literature pieces in the nature of news items.

Every couple weeks, you should release your latest endorsements with the prior endorsements scrolled to the bottom of your literature, mail, social media applications, or whatever the method of communication may be. The continuous and systematic release accomplishes a couple things. First, it is like a never-ending water torture for your opponent who will no doubt see your list peppering him or her week after week. But, more importantly, it creates a sense of momentum which hastens the band wagon effect.

This method is ripe for the retail politician who works the district intensely with personal voter contacts, but the same method can, and with success often is, used in national elections by surrogates and effective party committees at the local level. At the national level, endorsements from popular culture icons are usually accrued throughout the campaign. There are a variety of ways to use these endorsements, but the main goal is to communicate to the particular electorate that popular and likeable people have chosen you. If done effectively, the band wagon effect created can be difficult if not impossible to stop.

THE POWERFUL POSITIVE MESSAGE

Message development can be one of the most important aspects of a political campaign. The sophistication of message development will depend generally upon the level of campaign with which you are involved. The local, or small-town campaign will undoubtedly have an easier time identifying a message that resonates with the voters. Conversely, a large district or federal election will likely require a great deal of research to develop targeted messaging to multiple constituent groups. The small district election usually has most of the electorate on the same page when it comes to a local hot button issue. Any candidate is wise to gather feedback on the issues by the most effective means. Opinion polling or other surveys can help narrow down your message, or spending time at town hall or with a local government beat reporter may yield a great deal of information as to what the people are discussing in terms of local issues. Whatever your method of data gathering, messaging is a key component in any political election.

The essential pillar of messaging must include the development of a powerful positive message. The message should resonate with voters in a feel-good way. This is not to say that there should not be hard hitting contrast messages or even what some may call negative messaging, but those techniques are collateral election devices that should only be used by experienced political consultants and public relations experts. The central pillar of electoral messaging must be a firm, powerful and positive message about you or what you will accomplish when elected.

Your powerful positive message should be a message that would make your mother or father the *most* proud to see on television. By another measure, it should be the concept for which you would most like to be recognized at an awards ceremony. An overwhelming number of people assign likeability to feel good information. If you are producing a message that makes your average person emotional in a positive way, then you are likely hitting on the right message.

THE CHALLENGER'S MESSAGE

The challenger has the tougher path in terms of message development. He or she is in the position of trying to convince voters to change the status quo from an incumbent, yet must appear likeable, popular, and positive. This is a difficult balancing act, but one that he or she has signed up for by deciding to run against an incumbent. The challenger thus always must produce a powerful positive message for "change."

In arguing for positive change, the challenger must produce one powerful contrast communication piece that lays out the most potent issue in the race. There must be considerable time spent in finding the one issue that produces the most dissatisfaction with the incumbent. Too many specific charges against an incumbent, especially if they are "inside baseball" stuff make the challenger seem petty. In fact, the remaining complaints against an incumbent should be part of the whisper circuit and not an official part of the challenger's campaign.

One powerful contrast piece which displays the positive benefits of choosing the challengers solution is the best chance of defeating an incumbent and winning the campaign for "change." If a challenger has done their homework correctly, they will notice resonance with their message among voters. Do not let go of the message and do not alternate with other messages. Message confusion results in the voter's loss of attention. Ride your potent message as *the issue* in the race, and ride it all the way to Election Day. It is the challenger's best chance of turning back the natural power of incumbency. Do not produce it late in the campaign cycle lest the incumbent brushes it off as desperation on your part. Bring it out early and often. If it is indeed a powerful issue, the incumbent must explain it. If the incumbent fumbles the explanation, it means that you have found a true vulnerability, and it will not go unnoticed by either the press or the voters. Press them on the matter and don't let up by switching to other issues. There is a temptation for a challenger to gleefully rejoice in the fact that they have struck gold with a "change" issue and decide to break out other issues. The problem with this is that the incumbent no longer needs to explain the initial potent message point, and you have no guarantee that your other points will, in fact, resonate with the voters, and again, you may end up sounding like a malcontent. Find the powerful positive message point and stick with it.

MESSAGING IN AN OPEN SEAT ELECTION

The open seat election has the greatest flexibility in finding a powerful positive message, but also can be difficult due to a multitude of message options. Your goal here is to research and find several positive message points relating to as many constituent groups as possible. Remember, voters do not know you or your opponent all that much and thus they need enticement to your side. Elections are about numbers, and in particular, the concept of addition. Cobble together as many constituent groups as possible and find the issue that they most care about, and if you can do so in good faith, adopt their issue as yours. As you do this you will find instant supporters for your campaign. The key is to work hard to find as many such groups as possible and make sure not to adopt issues that you have no intention of pursuing once in office. Of course, this has been done before, but there is nothing in politics more malignant and hostile as a cheated constituent group. Many such groups will pursue your subsequent defeat later even having forgotten the specifics of your initial breach of promise. They will just remember that they hate you beyond words – but they will find words as well as energy to defeat your reelection or bid for a different office! The art of politics is the art of making friends within your particular political universe, and thus establishing a reliable base of support. The elected officials who do the opposite do not last long in the political arena.

MESSAGE OF THE INCUMBENT OFFICE HOLDER

If the challenger wants "change," then obviously the incumbent wants consistency. The incumbent campaigns on themes such as achievement, experience, reliability and tops it off with the insinuation that the challenger will take us backwards to a time of less progress or prosperity. The incumbent emphasizes whatever he or she can and has either the advantage or difficulty of having a record upon which to run. If the incumbent has enjoyed success with new programs or policies, they will be emphasized as a way of reminding the voter that the term of office of the incumbent has enjoyed success. The message is obviously why would we switch elected officials if there has been success by the current office holder?

NEGATIVE MESSAGING

Negative campaign themes are perhaps one of the most difficult message concepts to manage in a political campaign. This is perhaps true because there is no central definition of what constitutes a "negative" message. Obviously, a direct personal attack on a collateral non-issue in the campaign would not only be considered negative, but also would, in most instances backfire against the candidate directly using the tactic. However, many times a negative message is one that many people would consider "fair game" in a political contest. For example, pointing out that a congressional candidate failed to file federal income taxes in the past arguably bears upon the candidate's fitness for a federal office in which he or she may have to vote upon matters of taxation. On the other hand, such a candidate, in the absence of a good defense to an issue like this, may cry foul claiming that your nasty campaigning is a desperate personal attack. Much of how the issue of negative campaigning is received by the voters depends upon how the matter emerges within and is treated by the news media. Media bias in favor of the tax cheat will frame the issue as a negative attack whereas bias in favor of the candidate pointing out the tax issue of his or her opponent will no doubt seriously damage the tax cheat.

Most campaign consultants will advise that negative messaging, though condemned by most, is actually effective. The problem with this advice is that the times where negative campaigning has worked have involved very special situations and circumstances such that it cannot be claimed to be an effective tool as a matter of general practice. Negative messaging is like dealing with an explosive. It should never be used in the hands of an inexperienced or first-time candidate without expert advice and counsel. It has the potential to be a very volatile and unpredictable form of messaging and can seriously backfire on the user.

Negative messaging can only be effective if an issue that displays your opponent in a poor light is known or discoverable by you. Experts will advise you to conduct "opposition research" on your opponent(s). This is a good idea as a matter of research generally, but just because you find something negative about your opponent does not mean that you should use it in the campaign. If you use it at all, the first step would be to have your surrogates test the subject matter in a "whisper campaign" where nothing is published or stated on record, but reactions are gauged by word of mouth interactions with voters. A second step would be to commission a voter survey designed to produce reliable data on whether the issue you think is compelling is something that people care about. The most effective negative messaging is done through third parties particularly the news media. If a reporter believes the negative issue is legitimate, it is likely the information will come to light publicly without as much as a word from your campaign. This is true with lesser reliability if the third party is an online forum, blog, or other distribution source. Nonetheless, it is generally preferred that the candidate not use negative messaging as a formal campaign message point when surrogates or other third parties generally produce better results in distributing a negative message.

As a general principle, candidates should be prepared to defend against a negative attack by conducting opposition research on themselves- a concept referred to as "self-research." Look for your own vulnerabilities and have either an explanation for them or a claim of outrage against your opponent's tactics, or an appropriate measure of both. Have supporters primed to rush to your defense with some praising you and others decrying the "nasty" campaigning engaged in by your opponent. Then quickly move to your powerful positive messaging.

CAMPAIGN FINANCE AND TIME MANAGEMENT

Financing your campaign is the third crucial pillar of winning your election for public office. Your success in overseeing the financial aspects of the campaign is a major indicator as to your electoral success in general. The successful candidate should be aware that there are two major spheres of campaign finance with one being practical and one being legal. Both involve caution, but obviously the legal challenges associated with campaign finance pose the most intimidating aspects of the money issue of politics.

The new candidate for office should be aware that campaign finance law varies depending upon the office you seek. Federal office campaigns are overseen by the Federal Election Commission and are highly regulated. Your best bet in a federal election is to seek a professional campaign consultant who can guide you to an experienced treasurer who will navigate this landscape on your behalf. Absent this, a new federal candidate should seek out someone who has managed a federal campaign account successfully either for a federal party committee or other federal candidate.

State and local offices are covered by state law. Many states have exemptions for small district races of limited voter population. Thus, your first step in a local race of fairly small dimension is to determine if you are required by law to establish and maintain a campaign account that is subject to legal reporting and other requirements. Many states, as well as the federal government, have published candidate handbooks for finance laws and regulations that affect the race in which you may be involved as a candidate. These are extraordinarily helpful, but generally they come with a caution that such handbooks do not constitute legal advice and any questions or concerns of a significant nature should be referred to experienced legal counsel.

THE CAMPAIGN TREASURER

One of the first steps in declaring your candidacy for public office is to establish a treasury with a financial institution. Banks are aware of this and have great experience in helping set up these accounts. However, the candidate generally must select a treasurer and file with their electoral regulatory agency paperwork that discloses the fact of a campaign account and the identity of the treasurer. Some, if not all states, permit the candidate to simultaneously serve as candidate for office and their own treasurer. Most smart campaign consultants will tell you that even though this may be, depending upon state law, allowable it is a mistake for the candidate to also serve as treasurer. Moreover, many consultants will advise that you should not have a family member or relative serve in this position. The reason that is most often cited is that campaign finance reports are required to be filed in a public office and are discoverable by the public which of course means, your opponent will have open access to your reports. Campaign finance reports are combed over for mistakes or other issues and it is not uncommon for opposing campaigns to make very public complaints about your reporting. Either through a surrogate, or by way of the opposing campaign directly, it is not uncommon to claim that there has been illegality or other unlawful conduct in the handling of money. For this reason, it is generally advised that neither the candidate nor any family member should be anywhere close to the money or the reporting that is required in a campaign. Plausible deniability sometimes is the catch phrase for this concept. If a problem with reporting arises, the candidate always should be in the position of claiming that he or she has recognized and corrected the problem in a demonstration of leadership and organizational acumen typical of their talents or experience in management. Plus, it is easier to fire a treasurer to whom you are not related! The point is that a candidate should maintain a healthy distance from the money in their campaign whether it be in the receipt or expenditure of funds. In fact, when the day comes that you are working the front door of your fundraiser by greeting supporters, make sure that you politely direct them to the registration table when they extend their hand with an envelope containing contributions. Never let contributions touch your hand if possible, especially in a modern era where people can photograph or record your every move. You better believe that you will not like the image of you holding a check or envelope being displayed on your opponent's literature.

THE RESOURCE OF CANDIDATE TIME

Aside from money, the time of the candidate is valuable and indeed a limited precious resource. Even the most experienced incumbent has a difficult time limiting their contact with voters or other supporters. People generally have no concept that a public officer serves a multitude of people, and thus many people tend to trap the candidate in lengthy discussions and try to monopolize their time. The higher the office, the greater difficulty a candidate will have managing the time that they have relative to what they can practically spend engaging in voter contacts. There are a number of techniques that a candidate should remember in order to strike a balance between the good faith interaction with voters and supporters and the reality that they cannot spend too much time with any one person.

Consider your time to be a campaign asset and think of spending it the way a frugal money manager would allocate funds. First, get the most for your time just like, in financial matters, you would want the most "bang for your buck." If you have a chance to address multiple voters on a single occasion, then that is a good expenditure of your time. When you engage in one on one voter contact, allow your assistant to politely remind you in front of the voter that you have to get going in order to meet other or additional commitments. Practice your message points, so when you are finished saying your piece, the voters can respond with concerns. Make sure to listen, and to ask your assistant to take a note or two about the voter concern and politely make your exit. Ideally, you should spend just a few minutes per voter.

There is a finite number of minutes between your declaration of candidacy and Election Day. The successful candidate watches their time commitments just as much as they watch their funding. Both time and money, when well spent, equal votes.

BUDGETING

During your decision-making process, you should have framed out a basic financial budget that, based upon your research, constitutes the finances that you need to effectively campaign. Like any budget however, it is not uncommon for events and circumstances to cause a candidate to have to revisit the concept of a good budget. Given that you should be spending your time campaigning, delegation of duties, where possible is always an effective time management principle. Select, if possible, a "finance chair" of your campaign to handle both budgeting and fundraising. In a small campaign, this certainly could also be your treasurer, but at a certain level, the duty of budgeting and fundraising are simply too much to juggle with the duty of serving as an effective treasurer. In fact, in many large-scale campaigns a budget coordinator may also be different from the fundraising chair, but for most campaigns, one person can do both.

As a general matter, campaign budgets should account for the following possible expenses:

- Filing fees
- Banking costs
- Paid staff
- Accounting and legal services
- Direct mail marketing costs
- General postage costs
- photography
- Website construction
- Social media development and maintenance
- Newsprint advertising
- Web based advertising
- Video ads for television and/or internet
- Literature design and print costs
- Campaign signage
- Campaign apparel
- Voter contact database
- Voter list acquisition
- Telephone survey or polling costs
- Transportation expenses
- Campaign meals and lodging

The above is by no means an exhaustive list but is a decent framework around which a basic campaign budget can be developed. Of course, some items may end up being paid for with "in kind" contributions, which nonetheless must be accounted for in campaign finance reporting. Also, some budgeting strategy will consciously decide to forgo some items as not important to the election and thus not include them in the budget. Knowing what to assign for each category will require some consultation from persons familiar with campaigns or otherwise a professional consultant. Generally speaking, voter communication expenses are the most expensive. The greater the number of voters in your universe, the more you will need to spending in the attempt to communicate your campaign message.

CAMPAIGN FUNDRAISING

Fundraising is the campaign necessity that political candidates often despise. For a first-time candidate, soliciting money from others is an abhorrent task. Of course, fundraising is vital unless you are privileged enough to self-finance your own campaign. The vast majority of candidates will simply be required to fundraise. In the absence of devotion to this difficult task, you may will allow this vital pillar of electoral victory to collapse. This in turn will likely damage your campaign in a way that cannot be repaired. The candidate must accept the fact that they must fundraise, and that the candidate is the most effective fundraiser on board in the campaign. There are a number of principles that the candidate should consider so that fundraising is successful.

THE PERSONAL TOUCH OF THE CANDIDATE

In the majority of instances, the most successful fundraising is the candidate's personal solicitation of funds. By whatever method necessary, the first step in successful fundraising is for the candidate to personally ask for money. Either on your own initiative, or on the prodding of your campaign consultant, you will need to pick up the telephone and begin working your way through your list of friendly phone numbers and solicit contributions from your friends. This will no doubt include lobbyists with whom you deal as incumbent office holder, but the first-time candidate is unlikely to have that resource. So, the candidate will need to estimate a contribution amount from each friend that is close to what you think they may be able to contribute and ask for it personally. This should be followed with a thank you mailing with an enclosed envelop making it easy for them to send back a check.

The successful candidate will also target financially successful people in the particular district and seek an in-person meeting. This usually involves the high-level solicitation of funds that is preceded with some research on the target donor. Wealthy people are used to people asking them for money. Many will usually have a public track record on the Federal Election Commission or a state government website of how much money they have contributed to either a candidate or a cause. Cross referencing these sources of information can prove valuable to your campaign treasury. The successful candidate or their staff will have reviewed the campaign reports of past candidates, along with charitable giving recognition documentation with a view to discovering wealthy donors who may be sympathetic with the political views of the candidate. Mining the past donations to others can be a fertile source of campaign funds.

THE FINANCE COMMITTEE

Many candidates approach fundraising by recruiting a committee of financially successful persons willing to support the campaign. This theory spreads the duty of fundraising to generally successful people who are each tasked to raise a goal amount. The committee members, in turn, each delve into whatever fundraising method they choose in order to meet their promised guarantee. Generally speaking, such committee members will have their own network of similarly situated people upon who they call to make a contribution. Going through their lists of friends and business contacts, each committee member taps into their own base of financial contacts in support of the candidate they are assisting. This can be a tremendous method of fundraising as each committee member, in theory, will proudly compete against the other in order to not only meet their goal, but to exceed it by producing a generous portfolio of funds. The theory also suggests that a member who lags behind will simply write a check for the goal amount so as to not be outdone by the other members of the committee. In fact, some folks will take the hint that they are on the committee because they have wealth and will quickly proceed to writing a check rather than organize and host an event. If you are lucky to have this method of fundraising work, you will indeed be a political force with which to reckon as you will have this pillar of politics firmly supporting your campaign.

THE HOUSE OR VENUE PARTY STRATEGY

New politicians often make the mistake of renting a facility or hiring a reception organizer to host a gala or reception. This immediately involves costs and expenses for the campaign which generates excess overhead. A reception or party at a nice home of a supporter will not only save the expense of such an event, many times, invitees will attend an event for the chance to snoop around in the fine residence of another person. The successful candidate will not underestimate people's desire to attend an event at a supporter's large manor house that carries a local reputation for history or grandeur. Moreover, they will be willing to pay, if for no other reason, in order to visit the venue. The candidate will no doubt pick up supporters who may have been uncommitted and attended the event out of curiosity concerning the venue along with a passing interest in checking out the candidate. Your speech and voter contact will win them over, and your campaign will pocket their general admission fee.

THE "DRAW" EVENT

Another strategy for fundraising is to host an event with a featured speaker, artist, or musician. This will serve as an attraction that will draw people to your event. If the draw can be obtained as a contribution, then the candidate is ahead of the game. If not, at least one event sponsor should pay for the draw and receive recognition for their sponsorship. This allows the candidate to reach beyond the normal base of support to the next circle of potential supporters. The event can turn into not only a good fundraiser, but also a harvest of potential new grass root supporters who may volunteer for the many duties that will be involved in the campaign.

DIRECT MAIL SOLICITATION

Soliciting funds by mail is tough for beginners, but it is certainly possible. The initial concern for the average candidate considering a run for office is the assurance that funds will be produced that will cover the fees associate with the mail piece. Generally, the value in a mailing is not to net large amounts of funds from a mailing but to discover supporters and donors that you can foster a relationship with and turn into bigger donors to your campaign. The larger your electoral district, the more success you will have with obtaining lists. One strategy routinely employed is to produce mail pieces that resonate with a certain interest group and include within the piece the opportunity for the recipient to contribute. The theory behind this strategy is that members of identified interest groups have high motivation to support a particular cause that is important to them. If they receive a mail piece that demonstrates that you will fight for such cause or against a perceived evil they oppose, then their support for the cause will translate to support for you in terms of not only a vote, but also a financial donation. As you continue in your political career, you can grow your direct mail fundraising program over time to generate steady revenue for your campaign.

THE GALA EVENT

Perhaps the most time-consuming fundraiser is the "gala" or formal dinner event. This event carries obvious costs and expenses that will cut against the campaign fundraising profits. However, the gala can be an effective tool if a candidate has the time, money, organizational support, and a featured draw to assure that the event will be successful. The gala requires a great deal of advance sponsorships and ticket sales along with a well-executed invitation mailing and response card for acceptances, regrets, along with enclosed monies in either instance. The response card should not forget to include a place to submit a donation for a supporter who cannot attend but wishes to financially contribute to the candidate. A candidate using this strategy for a fundraiser may do well to work with someone who has experience bringing a gala to a successful fruition. There is nothing more discouraging than a poorly attended formal dinner except perhaps one that ends up costing the candidate money.

YOUR CAMPAIGN, YOUR INVESTMENT

One fundraising idea is to make your own personal investment in the campaign with a direct personal contribution that shows to your supporters that you also are financially invested in the effort to win public office. This investment displays confidence to your support base and makes them feel better about their own donation. Another personal investment, but with less significance, is a loan to the campaign made by you, the candidate. The value of this is the availability of additional funds if needed along with being able to carry the loan balance over past the campaign and repay the loan to yourself after the election regardless of the outcome. A significant loan also shows financial muscle on your campaign report, but make sure it is real muscle and not a flabby gesture on your part.

THANK YOU AND DONOR RECOGNITIONS

Aside from the basic concept of good manners, a heartfelt written thank you note is a must for a candidate. These should be written promptly so that not much time elapses between the donation and the expression of thanks. Donors also appreciate recognition on your event brochures, your web site and anywhere else that it makes sense to display the recognition of gratitude. A successful candidate know that you truly cannot say thank you enough for the kindness of a supportive financial contribution.

PILLAR FOUR

VOTER COMMUNICATIONS

The candidate may well have the greatest message in the history of politics, but if the voter never hears it, the message becomes meaningless. The fourth pillar of campaign victory is the ability to reach out and communicate to the masses. Your close friends and supporters know your message. In fact, your local political party committee may also know your message points verbatim. However, none of that is important because the people deciding on whether or not you win the election are the masses of people who don't really know you and likely have never heard you speak. In fact, they probably don't know a thing about you beginning with your name. Therein lies the challenge of communication with thousands, tens of thousands, or on the national scene, millions of strangers.

The final pillar of voter communication assembles all of that which you have prepared and executes the campaign by telling the voter why they must vote for you. Remember, money, message and popularity must be orchestrated along with a flawless communication strategy.

The First Mass Communication: Announcing your Candidacy

Very few first-time candidates for public office understand the importance of announcing that they are running for office. A prospective candidate will do well to remember that you never get a second chance to make a first impression. The announcement that you are running for office is the first time you will very likely reach a substantial audience of voters who will, for better or worse, form an initial opinion about you. For this reason, the successful candidate will prepare mightily for the campaign announcement.

Ideally, your announcement should include a blend of at least a portion of both your message and popularity pillars with some resonating message points and some potent endorsements that mean something to the voting universe. To do this effectively, you must determine which message points will likely make an initial impact on your audience. Prior work in the community in which you are running for office to discover and understand issues that people care about should be done well prior to the announcement. In fact, the possible message points should be vetted to a degree so that you are not wasting your opportunity to strike a chord with voters in your initial public announcement. In a perfectly executed campaign announcement, the successful candidate will have also already lined up popular and well-known people to lend endorsements and quotes to your campaign announcement. As much of your powerful, positive message that you can include along with the third party credibility of endorsements from well known, likeable people should be wedged into your announcement and hammered home with as much follow through as you can muster.

The news outlets that would cover your race should be contacted with press releases and even perhaps an advance, in person visit with the editor in order to elaborate on your campaign. News organizations need content, and political races are terrific fodder for news stories. The initial campaign announcement is virtually guaranteed free coverage in the news. "Free media" is a golden opportunity to communicate with the universe of voters and any time a candidate can get cost free coverage in the news he or she must take advantage of the opportunity. The initial announcement is at least one virtually certain instance that you will get free media. Don't let this opportunity be a failure, rather use it to its full potential.

In the political campaign world, we sometimes use the term "optics." What your initial campaign announcement looks like is important to the voter who may see it and the news organizations that will cover it. Your press release should be pristine and captivating. Your potency as a candidate for office should jump off the paper at the news editor and scream that you are a political force of a dynamic and promising nature. It should make the reader at least think you may well win the race, so they better get on the story with full attention.

The optics of popular support are also vital in the initial campaign announcement. If possible, the press release should capture enough attention to compel news reporters to attend your announcement rally and photograph all of the smiling and excited supporters who demonstrate how you are the popular person in the race. If you can rally friends and supporters to a venue such as the local courthouse steps or other prominent, recognizable local place, then you will most certainly have an excellent backdrop against which to make your announcement speech.

The initial announcement will likely be one of the most enjoyable moments of your campaign. You will be in the honeymoon phase of your relationship with the news media. In this phase, the media generally is delighted to cover a new political event and is not focused on any hard-hitting news.

LIST BUILDING & TARGETING YOUR WIN NUMBER

Your communications efforts must target a sufficient number of likely voters in your universe. You need not, and likely should not attempt to communicate with every registered voter in your electoral district. The fact is that only a percentage of registered voters will vote in any given election. Professional consultants often provide the voter analysis needed in a particular election district that will guide your communications strategy in terms of who to target and how to develop an identified list of known voters who have committed to your candidacy during the campaign. This route usually involves contracting with a software company where you and your volunteers can access a database and update your voter's records in real time. These services can end up being among the largest expenses incurred by a campaign but if used to their full potential can be instrumental in securing a victory.

In the absence of professional guidance, a candidate may simply procure the list of voters from their board of elections or registrar and begin list building from that document. Identifying your known voters is key to a turnout plan. The process of communicating your message during the campaign should result in a list of voters who have indicated that they intend to vote for you. During a campaign and while in office, candidates often develop and closely guard their lists of supporters and known voters. This information is valuable for communicating directly to your most important audience.

During the beginning of the campaign, you will want to comb through data from past elections to determine a "win number" which is simply the number of votes you need to achieve victory. Take into account what other races are on the ballot in order to project turnout and try to target a specific number you need in each voting precinct to achieve victory based on past performance in those areas. Professional consultant can help you determine a very precise win number. These numbers will be valuable to you on election night so you can gauge how you are doing in early-reporting precincts. Keep in mind that you don't need to, and likely will not, win every precinct and that "losing well" in some areas can be critical to your success.

GETTING OUT THE VOTE WITH YOUR GROUND GAME

A maxim of electoral politics is that a winning campaign is one that "identifies their voters and turns them out on Election Day." Your lists should be constructed over the course of a long campaign and should reliably inform you as to who supports you and who you will remind to vote on Election Day. This above all else, is the key to electoral victory.

Your campaign should, above all else, employ an aggressive "ground game" of door knocking and phone calls. You and your volunteers and staff should spend a vast majority of their time knocking on doors and calling voters. Early in election season you may start with your voting universe, which might be a list of every registered voter in your district, a list of past primary voters, or registered members of your political party along with voters not party registered. However you decide to begin, your campaign should be dedicated to dutifully contacting these voters multiple times throughout the campaign and recording if they are supportive of your campaign. This first stage of you ground game should also include helping supporters who are not registered to vote register, where it is important to study your local laws around voter registration. You and your volunteers should also follow up each interaction with a supporter by asking if they would like a yard sign or bumper sticker, more details on these items are discussed later in this section.

After spending many early months in your campaign identifying supporters. You will want to turn to getting out the vote of the supporters you have identified. A get out the vote plan is a critical Election Day strategy that the successful candidate will use to assure the numbers of voters needed to pull the lever actually show up at the polls. Sometimes referred to as "GOTV," get out the vote strategies include a number of devices and tactics that will push your voters to vote. A candidate cannot assume that just because the big day has arrived that people will actually show up to vote. Voter apathy is a chronic problem for our democracy. I have often said that "if voting were as easy for a voter as hitting their snooze button, then everyone would vote." However, voting requires a commitment from the voter to take a portion of their day, travel to their polling place and wait in line to vote. To combat this, you will want to spend the final weeks of the election only contacting those voters you have identified as supporters in your many months of voter contact. You should focus on doing everything you can to make it as easy as possible for the voter to cast their ballot. You should provide information on early voting and voting by mail, where applicable. On Election Day or any other time early voting is open you and your door knockers should employ the "knock and drag" technique, where you attempt to get the voter to come with you to the polls, this works best with elderly or disabled voters who may need a ride to go vote. You should also send your supporters contact information for them to contact your campaign if they need a ride to the polls.

COMMUNICATING WITH DIRECT MAIL

A new candidate may erroneously feel that newspaper or magazine ads are a superior communication tool. History has proven, that while it may be important to have some advertisement presence in the news media, it is far more effective to communicate with voters by direct mail. Mail has the advantage of placing your campaign message within a handful of items that a voter will actually touch, process, look at and either throw away or leave sitting around for other family members to look at prior to disposal. At a minimum, your name has been seen by one or more household members. If mail piece has been effectively prepared, it may actually be read and reviewed favorably by members of the household receiving the item. It is a great and effective communication tool when used correctly.

A mail piece should be designed with a number of key features in mind. First, the candidate must use the piece to raise their name recognition. Voters tend to vote for a name they know as opposed to one they do not know. Second, a well vetted, powerful positive message (pillar two) should be included in in short, simple language. Finally, the reverse of the piece can elaborate on the message, restate the candidate name, and provide information as to how a voter may get additional information, volunteer for the campaign, or donate funds to the candidate. The piece should have a professional layout and clean look. Voters can sniff out cheap, silly, or unprofessional work in a mail piece, and in such cases you have actually done your campaign significant harm. Most mail houses have graphic artists who are available to help you with layout and to an extent with message. If you have good financial resources, your professional consultant will already know the fundamentals of direct mail marketing for a candidate including vendors who can handle the job. In a smaller race, you may still get the help from the printing company or mail house because they have printed political mail for years and can advise a new candidate who is a neophyte to politics.

Your mail campaign, if sufficiently funded, can roll out several mailings to the whole district, or targeted mailings to identified groups of voters who may connect with a message. A candidate can also use different types of mail such as a postcard type piece as well as a letter inserted into an envelope. The advantage of the post card is that even though it may be quickly disposed of, the candidate name has been seen by the recipient. The advantage of a letter is the ability to elaborate on your messaging with a sincerely written letter. While some will not open the letter, many will, and in fact many people still read political mail from a candidate, particularly in a local election.

Check with your local postmaster about bulk mail permits and rates for political mail. Special postal rules apply for political mail and your postmaster or postal employee can generally walk a new candidate through those rules. Of course, if you have a larger, and particularly well-funded campaign, the mail house that you hire will take care of these details for you.

CAMPAIGN SIGNS

Campaign signs don't win elections, but their presence can show support across your district. Especially in local elections, having a complete lack of signage can scare off potential supporters who want to be associated with a winner. Showing weakness or lack of robust support by insufficient signage is another peril for a candidate. Thus, signs are one of many forms of voter communication.

In advance of declaring a candidacy, one consideration should be to develop sign locations along well traveled routes in the election district. These locations should be on private property and posted with the owner's permission. The new candidate should also be aware that some localities will have sign permit requirements. It can be embarrassing to start posting campaign signs and then get a notice that your campaign is in violation of a sign ordinance in the district. There is some question as to the constitutionality of sign ordinances in connection with signs being posted on private property, but in reality, do you want one of your first campaign issues to be a dispute over a minimal permit fee? Also, if your election district includes multiple localities, you will need to check permitting requirements in each locality, and yes, pay each fee.

Given that campaigns can run for months and in some cases years, the candidate needs to budget for signage for the entire election cycle and for sufficient signage at the polling places on Election Day. Running out of signs is almost as embarrassing as not having enough sign locations throughout your election district. You should check with experienced incumbents or activists in the district for recommendations as to sign quantity. Also, one should know that buying in bulk is a money saver, and if the design of your sign is smart, it can be used in subsequent reelection efforts after you win your race, so the initial expense is actually a longer reaching investment than it may seem at the time.

The experienced office holder knows that signs are meant to raise the candidates name recognition and to show, by their vast presence throughout the district that the candidate has formidable support. Given this truism, the experienced candidate or office holder also knows that *signs are meant to be read*. Many new candidates have lost focus of this fact by designing signs and other campaign collateral that are cluttered with too much information and are designed with a goal of being attractive instead of being read within the several seconds of time in which a voter's car passes by the sign location. The best sign is in white (or very light color) letters on a dark background. This "reverse" color scheme gives a pop to the candidate's name and can be seen from a longer distance. Block letter font is best as opposed to any type of manuscript font that is meant for up close reading. The last name of course should be emphasized but there is no harm trying to include a first name above and slightly off center to the left of the candidate's last name. The office being sought should be on the sign along with any legal disclosure requirements such as "paid for and authorized by (candidate or committee name)" that may apply to your jurisdiction. And for goodness sake, do not put your photograph on the sign unless you want to be the subject of great laughter among the political types in your district. Photos on signs are for real estate agents, not for political candidates. Save your photo for mailers, "palm cards", and your online presence. If you rent a billboard, then maybe you can get away with including your photo on your sign, but really that is a different animal than a yard or road sign.

Speaking of billboards, in rural areas, signs simply called four by eights (4x8's), which are the size of a standard sheet of plywood are often purchased by a candidate for farm fences and barns. These signs are expensive, but in rural districts are golden endorsements from the agricultural community. 4x8's are a strong communication to others that you are an established and formidable candidate with significant support from a key constituency. Remember to get advice from some established office holders or activists and buy in bulk if you can. Again, these signs, properly maintained are an investment that you can reuse in several subsequent election cycles for your reelection pursuits.

OTHER PRINT MEDIA: BUMPER STICKERS, LAPEL PINS, BROCHURES, PALM CARDS AND OTHER HANDOUTS

Obama Biden 2008 bumper sticker (2810891603).jpg" by
Dave Winer from USA is licensed under CC BY-SA 2.0

If you are in politics long enough you will eventually hear the old saying that "a bumper sticker is the equivalent of two hundred fifty dollars of advertisement money." Bumper stickers can be purchased in great quantity and for low cost, and a few can go a long way. A candidate should endeavor to get as many of these spread throughout the district as they can because, in terms of mass communication it is not only cheap, but effective. Lots of bumper stickers with your name on them traveling around town show significant popular support. People generally jealously guard their automobiles condition and the fact that they are willing to put your name on their car is significant. One tip is to get vinyl style "stretchy" stickers that remove easily so as to help your supporters get comfortable with putting a sticker on their car. Lots of people don't want to clutter their car or put stickers on their car even though they like you. You can persuade them by telling them these are "the expensive vinyl kind" rather than the "cheap paper and glue kind" and will come off the car very easily at the end of the election cycle. Have them with you any time you or a supporter will be interacting with voters and push them along with your literature. Also, remember, bumper stickers are a form of print media and are likely required to have an appropriate legal disclaimer. And, like yard/road signs they are meant to be read, not to be pretty. A good block letter reverse color design can be seen by 10 car lengths or more while a manuscript font can only be read at stop lights by the guy behind you in traffic.

Similarly, a lapel pin or sticker is also a form of print media and the same admonitions and advice apply to them. These items are best used at large political events where you will want it to appear as though many of your supporters are in attendance. However, since a pin or a sticker is meant to be read up close in a personal way, you can have a bit more freedom with your design. Remember that your basic design is also your "brand" and you want to have a certain level of consistency so that repetitive sightings of your brand allow it to be etched in the mind of those who see it. Your brand should be on all your voter communications from letterhead to mail pieces to lapel pins.

Brochures and palm cards are commonly used as direct handouts during parades, county fairs, door to door canvassing and other events. With this print media the candidate and volunteers have something to directly put in the hand of the voter with which you have come into contact. Brochures generally contain more information about the candidate and his message and come in a variety of folds. Your printer can help you format your candidate biography and your message points in the brochure in a way that is effective and visually appealing. The palm card is a scaled down version of your brochure. The card can be printed in a number of dimensions and is typically a two-sided information piece with your name, logo and branding prominently displayed along with a few message points and your contact information and website address.

During the campaign you will have opportunities to develop additional print materials for handing directly to voters. One classic campaign handout is the local high school sports schedule with your logo and name prominently displayed on a postcard style handout. You can even use a pro team schedule if your geographic district is near where the team is headquartered. Remember however, do not use logos of teams or schools without permission. With an effective and well-planned design, the sports schedule card may end up posted on the family refrigerator with a magnet. This guarantees prominent name display to the household voters for at least the duration of the sport season.

Another classic print media tip to push the candidate name is to wrap lapel stickers around water bottles given out at the county fair or at the July 4th parade during the steamy heat of summer. Not only is the water appreciated, but your name will be carried around by hundreds of thirsty voters. Since candidate lapel stickers are cheap and tend to be sold in rolls of 500, 1000 or more, this is a good way to get them out there to the voters rather than having several hundred left over after the campaign has ended. As with all print media, make sure that any applicable legal disclosure or disclaimer is included on the piece.

MEDIA RELATIONS

Writing a Press Release

The newcomer to electoral politics will be delighted to learn that there is one form of mass communication that is "free." If and when the news media covers you and your race, numerous voters will have the chance to finally pick up additional information about you and your candidacy. In this regard, the media can be a great resource in voter communication depending upon how well the candidate harnesses the power of the news media. For at least an initial period of time, the relationship between the candidate and the news media is symbiotic. They need content on a daily or weekly basis depending on their publication schedule and you need to reach the voter through their readers or followers. They need to fill up space with information and you need to publish information to your electoral universe. They have a readership base and you need a voter base. Sounds like a beautiful relationship, right? Well, for at least a time in can be. Setting aside issues of bias or favoritism and the concept of professional journalism, there are some realities that a candidate needs to know.

The press release is a tool to get your "story idea" concerning your candidacy to the editor or reporter of a given news outlet. There are numerous guides to writing a good press release, but a number of techniques and tips are available here that should guarantee you space in the paper or on their website.

First, your release should be no longer than a page and should be clear, concise and without mistakes. Get one or two proofreaders to review your release prior to sending it. A poorly written or grammar-challenged press release will assure that you have made a negative impression with the news outlet. A couple extra sets of eyes with good language skills can help keep your press release up to professional standards and taken seriously by the recipient.

Second, if you have a visual element such as a good candidate photo, or other graphic you should include it with your release. Visual elements are powerful aspects of communication that elevate the story that you are sending to the news outlet and make it more appealing. This helps both the chances of being published as well as perhaps the placement of your story within the publication. A great campaign promise, idea or message accompanied by good graphics can be enticing to an editor.

Third, as referenced above, an excellent press release will format the story for the reporter or editor. Writing the release in the third person in a narrative news story style shows the editor or reporter what the story will look like in print (or on the web). So, for example your release could begin by saying "hello, I have decided that I will support lower taxes if I am elected, can you please write a story about my position?" This of course is silly and amateurish, but you would be surprised by the number of newcomers to politics who simply don't understand how to write a press release. The same press release content would be immeasurably better stated with an introductory story lead-in as follows:

> *"Middletown, U.S.A. – September 28, 2024 Today, John A. Candidate stood before a throng of campaign supporters and other potential voters at Tammany Square and promised to lower taxes. The promise caused the assembled crowd to erupt with applause."*

The above example is simply meant to illustrate how a third person narrative in the news story style sets out what the story would look like in print. It is designed to show an editor how the piece will appear, and the accompanying content will help the reporter who may adopt the story idea such that it is practically already written. In fact, many local, small outlets will print your release as their story if it is clean and professional largely by cutting and pasting much of the content you have provided. This assures that you are not misquoted and that your message appears as you want it to appear. Of course, many reporters may take some of your language and adopt it but supplement and write the story based on the follow up phone interview with you as well as perhaps others who might contribute to the news piece. The point is that you will have gotten your name and a portion of your message out to the reader base of the news outlet for free.

The release should also have a proposed headline. In the above example, the candidate should format a news style headline at the top of the release that grabs the attention of the recipient. For example, the candidates headline in the release above could be "CANDIDATE PLEDGES LOW TAXES, CROWD THUNDERS APPROVAL." The successful candidate should research the many resources on how to write a good press release and under no circumstances should just start sending letters or emails to the news outlet expecting to garner publication of free media. Again, the advice of professionals can help greatly, but the principles expressed here cover the basics of a decent press release.

Meeting with Editors

A new candidate should endeavor to meet with the editors of each news outlet in the election district in which they are seeking election. When you ask for a meeting you should have already provided them with a well written biography and your candidacy announcement press release. An early meeting will help to establish rapport with the editor who will likely take the opportunity to ask questions about your candidacy. A candidate should be polite, respectful, and engaging with the editors in the district and ask to meet the staff reporters who may be covering the race. As with any meeting of persons you hope to convince of your likeability, you should follow with a professional and sincere thank you note that appropriately expresses your gratitude for the time that they have given to meet with you.

When identifying media outlets to reach out to about your candidacy, it is important to be as broad as possible. In addition to reaching out to traditional print and broadcast media, there are probably a variety of online community news sites and blogs that have a wide readership among your voters. This could also include political blogs, often run by state or local party activists, that will likely reach many voters in your party's primary. Be sure to identify and keep in contact with these media sources as well.

Some candidates will also take the time to provide additional campaign materials to the editors or reporters at the time of an initial meeting such as graphics, brochures and photography that they can use any time they cover you or your race. A successful candidate will likely have already engaged a professional photographer to take a portrait shot of the candidate and perhaps some family photos as well. Be aware that in the absence of you providing a photo to the news outlet, they will ask you for the opportunity to take a quick photo of you during your visit, or at some other time. This photo may not be the flattering photo you want associated with your campaign. The lighting will be poor and you pretty much are guaranteed a lousy photo, which will follow you during the campaign. It is not unheard of to ask an editor to use a substitute photo from one that has been used, and generally speaking, the news outlet will likely comply with your request. Of course, they are not obliged to do this, but in the interests of a compatible and harmonious relationship, it is not uncommon that an editor grants your request to associate certain photos with the stories on your campaign.

Advertising with the Media

A candidate should make it clear that they will spend valuable campaign dollars advertising with the news outlet. In fact, a common tactic is to inquire with the editor early as to how you can reserve premium advertisement space either in the print portion of their news or on their internet news site. In fact, news organizations are rapidly shifting to online news and advertising. In doing this, most organizations sell "pop up" ads as well as premium ad banners on their website pages including their individual posted news stories. So, a candidate should find out early how to reserve the premium banners and pop up or "rollover" ads so that around election time your name and candidacy is prominently displayed to the readers of the site.

It would be a good idea to have a budget for an initial advertisement flurry around the time of your announcement and meeting with the editor. This shows the editor that you are a serious candidate as well as one who is organized enough to have planned for some initial expenditures that coincide with the launch of the campaign. It also alerts the news outlet that they will earn income from your race such that they should treat you fairly and respectfully lest you pull your ad reservations and reallocate your money to another news organization. Of course, the initial flurry of ads will subside as the campaign is long and campaign funds are precious. However, this early investment along with advance reservation of space will pay off later during the campaign.

Communicating with Voters by Phone and At the Door

As discussed earlier in this section, the candidate should spend the vast majority of his or her time talking to likely voters via phone or in person by door knocking. It may be considered "old school" campaigning but speaking with voters by telephone and in person by door knocking still remain the most effective means of gaining support. The smaller your election district and the smaller your universe of likely voters, the easier time you will have contacting your entire universe of voters. Many local races involve at least a portion of the district that is rural or semirural so a delicate balance of both door knocking and phone calls is effective as well as an efficient use of the candidate's valuable resource of time.

A successful candidate will know that courtesy and humility is a needed combination for such personal campaigning. A phone call or knock on a voters door can be intrusive and in the absence of basic politeness and a humble approach by the candidate, or a candidate's, voters can be annoyed and less likely to voter for your side. The last thing a candidate wants is a "backfire" on a communications technique where they have ended up losing votes. So, all the elements of good manners need to be at full attention when interacting with voters.

A very important point in the concept of humility and courtesy is the commonsense observation that while the candidates time is a precious resource, so is the time of the voter who you are speaking with. While some voters will be engaging and want to talk for a while, most will want to end the interaction quickly. So, you have about a minute or less to emphasize your name, the office you are seeking, a few message points as well as your basic sincerity as a candidate. You must think through your very quick remarks ahead of time, even writing down your remarks and practicing their delivery. Many candidates assume that because they are speaking with a voter, they can just take as much time as they want and sometimes horrifyingly the candidate will launch into their stump speech that is meant for an assembled crowd. Instead, the successful candidate will make their quick remarks and end the conversation with a sincere invitation to the voter to give the candidate "some advice" on what the voter feels is important to them. The approach of trying to get the voter talking to you about what is important to them can garner respect, appreciation and a virtual guaranteed vote from that person and their household members on Election Day. Additionally, this approach can end up being the most valuable opinion poll you can take. If you start to hear the same concerns from voters, you will potentially have harvested a powerful message point (Pillar two) for your campaign to emphasize to the entire electoral district.

After a while, you, the candidate, or your appropriately trained volunteer will get comfortable with talking to voters. You will quickly learn how to navigate through a standard voter interaction as well as how to handle people hanging up on you or slamming the door in your face. Don't sweat the negative interactions. If a voter hangs up on you rudely, they either were not a likely voter anyway, or they were already in your opponent's camp, and in such case they have saved you time by ending the phone call. Additionally, your negative interactions allow to collect valuable data on who is not supportive, so you don't have to waste time interacting with that voter during the remainder of the campaign. You will quickly learn to just move on to the next voter and after a while, you will develop a comfort level that makes campaigning a breeze. If you get to a voter who has so much time on their hands that they begin to monopolize your time by non-stop talking, find a way to move on. This affords you the chance to learn how to politely extract yourself from a conversation with a "I'm so sorry, I have to let you go because my other line is ringing, thank you again for your valuable time and I hope we have a chance to catch up later, bye now." The polite extraction is also a skill that you will develop and after a while it will become perfectly natural. Finally, you, the candidate should have a thoughtful and concise voicemail in the very common event of a non-answer at the voter's home. Remember, your voice is being recorded, so a brief, sincere message is what you want preserved in their voicemail.

Volunteers are a valuable way to multiply your campaign efforts. However, volunteers who campaign for you are your representative and while talking to voters are the voice of your campaign. A candidate must spend time with their volunteers and train them with some simple protocols prior to setting them loose on the voters in the district. First, the rules that apply to the candidate regarding politeness, humility, disengagement, and the handling of rude voters, also apply to the volunteer. Second, your volunteers should be on a short leash and given a script to follow that is well thought out ahead of time. The script should include a version in which a message can be left on an answering machine or service that emphasizes the candidates name, message points and an invitation to look up the candidates website as well as a call back number in the event an interested voter would like more information or even if they would like to volunteer for the campaign. The exigent circumstances that may arise during a phone call should be covered in campaign training and monitored by the candidate to assure the troops are staying on message and not costing you votes.

Robocalls

Another technique in modern campaigning is the use of "Robocalls", which are automated phone calls that have a mixed acceptance in political circles. Some folks praise the method but there are those who are convinced that robocalling simply turns off voters who are annoyed with such phone calls. If you can find a middle ground that does not overuse this tool, it can reap rewards for your campaign. Automated calls at the beginning of a campaign may be an easy way to gather information from your election district about what issues are resonating with the voters. Are they concerned about taxes, school funding, transportation; just what is the hot button issue in your locality if any? An automated call from the candidate should be no longer than 30 to 45 seconds that introduces your name, message points and a reference to where the voter can get further information about your campaign. Finally, a few well-timed and well-scripted automated calls as an effective GOTV strategy in the final hours of a campaign to urge their identified supporters to make it to the polls. Robocalls can dial tens of thousands of phone numbers with the candidate's plea for support and votes within several minutes. Third party robocalls can also be effective if you have a well-known supporter who can call on your behalf, again with a brief 30 second message of support. While automated calling has gained some criticism, many successful candidates will tell you that, if used strategically and in moderation, these calls constitute an effective and powerful communication tool to touch large numbers of voters simultaneously with your message.

Consultants will also tell you about automated interactive calling in what is sometimes referred to as a "tele-town hall." At a relatively inexpensive cost, automated calls can be made to thousands of voters who are invited to join your live, "town hall" style candidate forum where the candidate will make a brief introduction with message points and open the phone lines for questions from the "audience." The system of the vendor who provides the automated service will place caller questions in que and the candidate can select from the que which questions to field. Usually, a candidate will stage at least a few calls from supporters to assure that message point questions are asked that the candidate can field with ease. This method of calling also can be quite effective because thousands of voters can be engaged simultaneously. Again, moderation is important as voters can quickly get turned off by repetitive phoning to their residence.

DIGITAL COMMUNICATIONS

The digital field has grown to become a major communications tool in modern political campaigns. What began as traditional mass email campaigns has grown to envelop email, social media, geo-targeted smartphone advertising, digital video ads, and more. The data that is collected and utilized in these operations has become a multibillion-dollar global business. The growth of the digital field makes some sort of online presence necessary for even the smallest campaigns.

The beginning of your digital communications strategy should be email. A robust email list allows for mass engagement. You should try to collect the email addresses of all supporters you speak with and talk to other supporters of your campaign about borrowing their email lists. Modern email platforms are numerous and walk even the least technologically savvy campaigner through sending out professional looking HTML based emails. Every major development in your campaign or press release that you send to the press, should also be sent to your supporters via email as should regular campaign newsletters. That being said, the use of email should also be balanced and complimented by your social media presence.

Your social media accounts should be created prior to announcing your candidacy. While there are numerous social media platforms, you should at least begin by creating a twitter and Facebook profile for your campaign. Most of your social media activity should be profiling you attending various campaign events to give the impression that you are running a very active campaign. Major announcement, policy positions, and messages should also be quickly summarized on your social media accounts, with a link to a longer article or webpage. It is also important to limit who has the ability to post from your accounts to just one or two of your most trusted staffers or volunteers. You should also set guidelines with these individuals about what kinds of posts will require your approval.

With the continuing prominence of social media, a candidate may be tempted to disregard email as a communication method. This is a mistake. In the world of political communication, the candidate needs to have a presence on all forums without exception. While email communication has diminished, it is still used by a significant number of voters. So, the candidate must, in terms of communication, be everywhere as often as possible in order to reach the maximum number of voters in the election district. Mass email communication platforms remain an important consideration for the successful candidate. In fact, most programs permit the compatible use of email with social media such that an emailed message can also be linked to social media.

So, a serious candidate will search out lists from political colleagues and associates and build lists of their own. Lists however can be proprietary and subject to rules regarding spam so one must observe the requirements of your mass email provider scrupulously. Mass email providers also have tools that help candidates build their lists legitimately. Generally, most providers will require that you affirm that the persons on your list have your permission to include them. They also will monitor complaints from recipients as well as spam reports. If your emails draw too many such complaints, you may lose your account with the provider. Again, as with all media, there is likely a disclaimer or disclosure requirement for political campaigns that should be included on all email messages in accordance with your local law.

YOUR WEBSITE

A professional looking website has become an expectation in campaign communications. It can, and indeed should, become your online communications hub where you can store multiple and varied message points about yourself and your campaign. In fact, it can be a single location where you host detailed information that would be too voluminous and time consuming to put into a brochure, video commercial or phone call. This will be an area that a particularly curious voter can go to get answers, and careful scripting can detail many explanations about the ideological platform upon which you are seeking voter approval and election to public office.

Your website should include a biography page in which you share your life's story along with your qualifications and credentials. Your bio should include an effort to humanize and popularize yourself (Pillar One) and your candidacy. It is preferable to write it in the third person context. Include your positive message (Pillar Two) in a way that is complemented by your unique experience, education, training, and other credentials for the particular office.

Your website should also include an online donation page, and a sign-up page for volunteers to join the campaign. Since websites are a communications hub, you should also assure that there is a function for the voter to make contact and ask questions of the candidate, and even seek further materials such as yard signs or bumper stickers and other promotional materials. You should also make every effort to have your website and donation page live at the time of your announcement so curious voters who read about your announcement can learn more about you and your friends and supports can make an immediate initial donation.

Your website can, if you choose, host a blog feature of posted articles written by you as well as campaign volunteers. If you choose this feature, be aware that software applications that have a news or blog style feature usually are defaulted to permit comments to be posted. You will have to decide to welcome comments that you can respond to or mediate commentary on posted articles. Settings options or compatible plugins will permit you to adjust such defaults event to the point of hiding the author of the original article so that all articles have the appearance of being drafted news style in the third person context without attribution to a particular author.

Professional websites prepared by vendors can cost thousands of dollars, but with some study, most campaigns can be able to easily create good looking and functional websites that are sold by various vendors that will offer design templates, domain names, and technical support for your website products. The larger and well-funded campaigns may opt for professionally programed websites, but many local offices are captured by a successful election that used self-created websites and volunteer help of technically oriented workers.

COMMUNICATIONS FOR INCUMBENTS

If you have been successful in your initial campaign, it is important to remember that every action you take while in office will affect your chances of reelection. The greatest advantage that incumbents have is that they can use the "bully pulpit" of their office to interaction with their constituents and show that they are an effective leader who is delivering on campaign promises. It is important to remember that "constituents" and "voters" are essentially interchangeable terms and you should treat each as the other. A successful incumbent will make sure that he or she is continuing to visit local clubs and associations even when they are not campaigning for reelection in order to hear feedback and remain visible in the community and positive in your public profile.

The most important way to remain popular as an incumbent is to deliver top=notch constituent services. Constituents will come to you with any variety of complaints or questions, many, or most of which may very well be out of the scope of your office. But you should take a lead on directing them to the right person to talk to and make notes of all your constituent interactions so you can follow up with them. Other constituents will reach out to voice their opinion on an issue or ask for assistance with a state or federal agency, often will may very well be able to help constituents navigate the complexities of government, in which case you will want to make sure you are responding to requests as quickly as possible.

When a constituent calls or writes you to voice an opinion contrary to yours, you should still respond and make them feel as though their opinion has been heard. Many of the skills you have gathered while talking to voters on the campaign trail will inform your ability to navigate interactions with disgruntled constituents and you should use the same principles of respect and politeness when dealing with these individuals.

You will want to also create an official newsletter for your office separate from your campaign that you can share information with your constituents through. Based on local rules, you can use your campaign email list as an initial list to grow your official mailing list from. Based on the office you hold, you might even consider creating separate social media accounts for your official use to keep you content separate from your political accounts. For legal and ethical reasons you will want to make sure you never use official resources for explicit campaigning, but that is not to say that you can't highlight he positive things you are doing in office through your official communications.

As you continue your career as an elected official, the basic communications skills learned from this pillar and skills learned from other sections of this book should be heeded in the same manner they were when you were a first-time candidate for office.

CONCLUSION

Following the principles of pollical campaigning set forth in this book will greatly increase your chances of attaining victory on Election Day. The details expressed are by no means exhaustive but hopefully after asking yourself the ten questions to see if you are ready to run for office, and synthesizing the four pillars, you are ready to embark on your campaign with eyes wide open.

As y0u can see there are many things to consider when you are weighing a run for elected office. If you determine it is a worthy undertaking, then you should approach your run for office with an earnest desire to do good for your future constituents.

The four pillars discussed in this book are completely dependent on one another your finances (Pillar Three) must allow you to communicate (Pillar Four) to the voting universe that you have a powerful positive message (Pillar Two), and, most importantly, that you are the popular (Pillar One), likeable person with whom the majority of people want to be associated. If you take away any pillar, the campaign likely collapses and fails. When all your pillars stand together, they support a successful, winning campaign.

ABOUT THE AUTHORS

Prior to his appointment as a Circuit Judge in Northern Virginia, James P. Fisher was a trial attorney in the courts of the Commonwealth as well as Federal Courts in Virginia's eastern district for over thirty years. He served two terms as elected prosecutor, as well as three terms as a local political party chairman where he managed and consulted on hundreds of political campaigns for public office. Prior to assuming the bench, he co-authored this work with his son Wes, a successful lobbyist and political consultant. Having witnessed campaigns for office overwhelmingly succeed, as well as those which failed miserably, this book is, in part, his "insiders" view of electoral campaigns with lessons learned. While it can serve as a catalogue of key reminders to incumbents, this book is also designed to teach the basics of winning campaigns to the political newcomer.

J. Wesley Fisher is a Virginia-based government relations and political affairs professional. He has served in a variety of full-time and volunteer roles on dozens of political campaigns and has built relationships with hundreds of elected officials across the nation. He currently manages state and local government relations for a national trade association in the Washington, D.C. area.

* 9 7 9 8 6 3 8 1 7 6 3 2 7 *